How to Be a SAMURAI

by Nel Yomtov

PEBBLE
a capstone imprint

Pebble is published by Capstone,
1710 Roe Crest Drive, North Mankato, Minnesota 56003
capstonepub.com

Copyright © 2026 by Capstone. All rights reserved. No part of this publication may be reproduced in whole or in part, or stored in a retrieval system, or transmitted in any form or by any means, electronic, mechanical, photocopying, recording, or otherwise, without written permission of the publisher.

Library of Congress Cataloging-in-Publication Data is available on the Library of Congress website.

ISBN: 9798875226854 (hardcover)
ISBN: 9798875234439 (paperback)
ISBN: 9798875234446 (ebook PDF)

Summary: Journey back in time to the Land of the Rising Sun and become a samurai! Learn about the armor, weapons, and traditions of these legendary warriors and find out if you have what it takes to become one of Japan's fiercest fighters!

Editorial Credits
Editor: Alison Deering; Designer: Bobbie Nuytten; Media Researcher: Svetlana Zhurkin; Production Specialist: Whitney Schaefer

Image Credits
Alamy: Aflo Co., Ltd., 17, Classic Image, 27; Bridgeman Images: © Look and Learn, 5, Stefano Bianchetti, 10; Getty Images: AFP/Kazuhiro Nogi, 13, duncan1890, 9; Newscom: Album, 7; Shutterstock: adolf martinez soler (stone wall), cover and throughout, anek.soowannaphoom, cover (top), Dongseun Yang, 11, hayakato, 21, Jean-Michel Girard, 29, Josiah_S, 15, metamorworks, 12, 14, 23, Picture Partners, 25, Rawpixel, 16, RPBaiao, 24, siriwat sriphojaroen, 18, Total art, 19, Warm_Tail, cover (bottom right), Yip Po Yu (texture), cover and throughout

Any additional websites and resources referenced in this book are not maintained, authorized, or sponsored by Capstone. All product and company names are trademarks™ or registered® trademarks of their respective holders.

Printed and bound in China. PO 006276

Table of Contents

Introduction
Japan's Fierce Warriors 4

Chapter 1
Are You Tough Enough? 6

Chapter 2
A Samurai's Weapons 14

Chapter 3
The Samurai Lifestyle 20

Chapter 4
The Fight Is On! 24

Test Your Samurai Knowledge! 30

Glossary 31

Index 32

About the Author 32

Words in **bold** are in the glossary.

Introduction

Japan's Fierce Warriors

Samurai were the famous warriors of Japan. They were highly respected in Japanese society. These expert fighters worked for powerful lords called **daimyo**. Each lord had hundreds of samurai. They protected the lord's territories against his enemies.

The samurai class of warriors began in the 12th century. They continued until roughly 1868. Over time, samurai joined together to form **clans**. The clans fought one another for control of Japan.

Do you have what it takes to become one of history's greatest warriors? Let's travel 500 years back in time to Japan and find out!

Chapter 1

Are You Tough Enough?

In the early years of the samurai tradition, any man could become a samurai. All he had to do was perform well in battle and show loyalty to his lord. But by the 1500s, a man could only become a samurai if his father was a samurai.

You are one of the lucky few. Your father is a samurai. Your training begins at age seven. Your father and the educators he hires will be your teachers.

Your training includes riding and caring for horses. You will learn to fire a bow while on horseback. You will also learn how to knock an opponent off his horse as he rides by.

You practice using swords, first with a wooden sword and later with real weapons. To develop hand-to-hand combat skills, you practice wrestling. You'll even be taught how to tie up prisoners using different knots.

Tip #1
Horseback Attack

To sharpen your archery skills, you'll ride a horse while wearing full armor. Your horse will gallop down a riding path or across a field. Then you'll fire your arrows at three small wooden targets mounted on tall poles.

Academic studies and mental training are also part of your education. You will learn to read and write. You will study math, literature, history, and poetry. You'll be more educated than the rest of Japanese society. Your knowledge will make you a good warrior and a strong leader.

shogi

Your teachers also have you play games such as go and shogi. These two board games are like chess. They will help you develop strategies that you'll need on the battlefield.

11

You work and study hard. At about age 13, you receive your first real sword and a suit of armor. This is done at a special ceremony called genpuku. It marks your passage from a boy to an adult man.

You'll also receive a new name from your lord or father. It is a combination of your father's name and a new name of your own. Congrats, young samurai! You are ready to serve your lord.

Chapter 2

A Samurai's Weapons

Your main weapon is your sword. You carry two swords into battle. The katana is about 2 feet (61 centimeters) long. The wakizashi measures about 1 foot (30 cm).

katana

You also use a long spear called a yari. It has two blades. You use this to keep your enemies at a distance and to attack them one by one. Your naginata is about 5 feet (1.5 meters) long. This weapon is made to sweep and thrust at opponents.

naginata

Only samurai are allowed to ride into battle on horseback. If your daimyo orders you to ride, you will arm yourself with a bow and arrows.

Some samurai clans have begun to use a long gun called an **arquebus**. Many older clans think it is not proper for a samurai to use a gun. Your daimyo will decide if your clan will use them or not.

In combat, you wear armor called **okegawa do**. It weighs about 45 pounds (20 kilograms). It is made of metal plates held together by **rivets**.

The armor covers your upper body, thighs, shins, and forearms. You decorate it with silver and gold. This helps to show your standing in society.

Under your armor, you wear a one-piece garment. This is covered by a short **kimono** and baggy pants. You also wear a metal helmet. It has flaps hanging down to protect your ears and neck.

Tip #2: Mind Games

Play mind games with your enemy! Wear menpo—scary face armor carved to look like an evil sea monster or an angry demon. This offers protection and also strikes fear into your enemies during combat.

Chapter 3

The Samurai Lifestyle

Your daimyo pays for your service with food, gifts, and land. He also gives you a place to live. Your home is in a large castle he owns. The rooms you live in are comfortable. They are decorated in wood and painted plaster. A moat and high walls surround the castle for protection.

You farm a small plot of land on the castle grounds. You grow additional vegetables to meet your needs.

As a samurai, you must follow a special code of conduct. This is known as **Bushido**. This means "the way of the warrior."

Your first duty is to be loyal and serve your daimyo. In all you do, you are required to show courage and honesty. You must live an honorable and moral life.

You may choose to retire from fighting when you can no longer serve your lord effectively. Or you may choose to move to another area of service. Until then, you are a samurai warrior. You must answer the call of battle.

Tip #3: Calm Your Mind

Being calm and relaxed is the key to your success as a samurai. **Meditate** every day. Quiet thoughts and deep thinking will keep you calm and loose. It will help you master your emotions.

Chapter 4

The Fight Is On!

Your lord orders an attack on a **rival** clan. It will take several days to reach your enemy's land on foot. You carefully pack your weapons. You also prepare your equipment and supplies.

Your main food is rice balls. These precooked goodies make a filling meal. During your long march, you'll also catch fish in streams and hunt for rabbit and deer. You'll gather whatever vegetables you can while on the move.

It is time to set off. You wear your armor all the time. This helps cut down on the amount of clothing you must carry. A rolled-up mat slung over one shoulder serves as your bedding.

Rest is not easy. You sleep in stables, under trees, and in farmhouses. You carry a canteen of water, medicine, and a pair of spare sandals in pouches hanging from your belt.

The day of battle finally arrives. Enemy warriors surround their lord's castle. They will fight to the death to defend it.

Your daimyo orders his samurai to seize the castle. You and your fellow warriors charge furiously. Soon, you're locked in a one-on-one battle. Your opponent lunges at you. You knock his weapon out of his hands with a quick swipe of your katana.

You raise your sword to deliver a deadly blow. But an enemy soldier suddenly appears behind you . . . how will the day end?

Tip #4: Watch Out!

Beware of **ninjas**! The enemy daimyo has hired these highly trained martial arts fighters to scout your army's position, steal your battle plans, and kill your daimyo. Stay alert!

Test Your Samurai Knowledge!

1. The powerful lord you work for is called a:
   a. chief
   b. daimyo
   c. big shot

2. What is your main weapon?
   a. sword
   b. rifle
   c. yari

3. What is mempo?
   a. an ancient Japanese form of self-defense
   b. a member of a rival clan
   c. a type of mask and face armor

4. Living according to Bushido is to:
   a. care for garden shrubs and bushes
   b. be honorable and loyal to your daimyo
   c. gain wealth and power

5. A genpuku ceremony celebrates:
   a. the Japanese New Year
   b. the birth of a new child
   c. the passage from boyhood to adult man

Answers: 1) b, 2) a, 3) c, 4) b, 5) c

If you answered all the questions correctly, you are ready to be a samurai! If not, take another read through this book and try the test again!

Glossary

arquebus (AHR-kwuh-buhs)—a long gun dating from about 1400

Bushido (BOO-shi-daw)—Japanese code of honor that demands unquestionable loyalty and obedience and places honor before life

clan (KLAN)—a large group of families and related people

daimyo (DY-mee-oh)—a nobleman of Japan who owned a great deal of land

kimono (kee-MOH-noh)—a long, loose robe with wide sleeves and a sash

meditate (MED-i-tayt)—to relax the mind and body by a regular program of mental exercise

ninja (NIN-juh)—someone who is highly trained in Japanese martial arts and stealth; ninjas were often used as spies.

okegawa do (oh-kay-GA-wa DOE)—a style of samurai armor made of metal plates

rival (RYE-vuhl)—someone with whom you compete

rivet (RIV-it)—a metal bolt or pin that is used to hold together metal

samurai (SAH-muh-rye)—a skilled Japanese warrior who served one master or leader

Index

armor, 9, 12, 18–19, 26

Bushido, 22

clans, 4, 17, 24

daimyo, 4, 6, 12, 16, 17, 20, 22–23, 24, 28, 29

education, 6, 10, 11, 12

family, 6, 12
farming, 20
food, 25

games, 11
genpuku, 12

horseback riding, 8, 9, 16
housing, 20, 26

meditation, 23
menpo, 19

naming, 12
ninjas, 29

retirement, 23

society, 4, 10, 18

time period, 4, 5, 6
training, 6, 8, 9, 10, 12

weapons, 8, 9, 12, 14–15, 16, 17, 24, 28–29

About the Author

Nel Yomtov is an award-winning author of children's nonfiction books and graphic novels. He specializes in writing about history, current events, biography, architecture, and military history. He has written numerous graphic novels for Capstone, including the recent *The Wright Brothers Take Flight*, *The Christmas Truce of World War I*, and *D-Day Training Turned Deadly: The Exercise Tiger Disaster*. In 2020 he self-published *Baseball 100*, an illustrated book featuring the 100 greatest players in baseball history. Nel lives in the New York City area.